KT-132-942

Color Your Life with Crystals!
Your First Guide to Crystals, Colors and Chakras
Margaret Ann Lembo

COLOR YOUR LIFE WITH CRYSTALS!

Your First Guide to Crystals, Colors and Chakras

Margaret Ann Lembo

Photography by
Andy Frame

EARTHDANCER

A FINDHORN PRESS IMPRINT

Publisher's Note

All information in this book has been compiled according to the publisher's best knowledge and belief. People react in different ways however, and therefore neither the publisher nor the author can, for individual cases, provide a guarantee as to the effectiveness or harm-lessness of the applications described herein. In cases of serious physical or mental health concerns, please consult a physician, alter-native practitioner, or psychologist.

First Edition 2013

Margaret Ann Lembo
Color Your Life With Crystals – Your First Guide to Crystals, Colors and Chakras

Copyright © 2013 Earthdancer GmbH
Text copyright © Margaret Ann Lembo 2012

Editing: Claudine Eleanor Bloomfield
Proofreading: Tony Mitton

All rights reserved. No part of this book may be reprinted or reproduced or utilized in any form or by any electronic, mechanical, or other means, now known or hereafter invented, including photocopying and recording, or in any information storage or retrieval system, without per-mission in writing from the publisher.

Cover Design: Dragon Design UK
Cover Photography: © Peter Fernau (young girl), © Nikki Zalewski/fotolia.com (crystals)
Photo model: Emilia Rother

Typesetting and graphics: Dragon Design UK
Typeset in Minion

Printed and bound in China

ISBN 978-1-84409-605-3

Published by Earthdancer GmbH, an imprint of:
Findhorn Press, 117-121 High Street, Forres, IV36 1AB, Scotland
www.earthdancerbooks.com, www.findhornpress.com

Contents

Dedication

To all the children of the world!
For all parents everywhere!
To all my cousins, nieces and nephews whom I love so much.

Acknowledgements

First, I give all of you who will read this book, a big THANK YOU! I have appreciation for all the children who have come into my store, The Crystal Garden, over the past twenty-four years asking me about crystals, gemstones, and rocks. It is because of their curiosity and attraction to the sparkling stones that I wrote this book. It's always a gift when a publisher believes in your project. I want to thank Sabine Weeke of Findhorn Press for introducing me to Arwen Lentz, the publisher of their imprint, Earthdancer. I am eternally grateful that you both had the vision to know that the young readers of our world need the information within these pages. Gratitude! Gratitude! Gratitude!

I had many teachers and mentors when I was little who taught me the power of positive thinking. I would like to give gratitude to all my teachers, mentors and colleagues who have shared their knowledge and wisdom with me. I acknowledge all the authors who have written self-help books and books on crystals.

I want to thank my friend, Lisa Paolo, and her children, for taking the time to go through this book a page at a time to make it child-friendly and easy-to-read. Likewise, I have so much gratitude for my cousins, Leala Dickenson and Alissa Gulisano-Waldman, who also took the time to comb every page and come up with great ideas for kids to enjoy this book. Thanks to them the activity part of each chapter is included to make it easier to integrate all that this book teaches and shares.

A special artistic thanks goes to Andy Frame of Andy Frame Photography. It is because of his great photographic talent that there are so many beautiful photographs of my gemstone collection throughout this book. Thanks to his wife and children for their hand in this photography project as well.

Of course, I have deep gratitude for the staff of The Crystal Garden, my bookstore, gift store and spiritual center. It is because of their dedication to running my retail store that I could take the time away from my business to write this book.

As always and forever, I am profoundly and lovingly grateful to my beloved, Vincent Velardez. His constant support, encouragement, and easy-going nature helps me every day to be all that I can be. Thanks, honey!

Introduction

This book is about how to use crystals, minerals, rocks, gemstones and metals to help you in school, with friends, with your emotions, and in all parts of your life. The book is an easy guide to gemstones based on metaphysical principles. The word "metaphysical" means that which goes beyond the physical. Metaphysics includes that which the physical and scientific world cannot define but we know exists.

This book is also a book about the power of positive thought, the power of your imagination, and the fact that thoughts are things. Improve your life by using these principles and combining gemstones with good thoughts. Use the teachings you will learn here and use them for the rest of your life. There is magic in believing! This book will teach you how to use the power of your belief, thoughts and your imagination to create whatever you wish to create in your life. You can use these tools to make good friends, do well in school, be happy and safe, and have high self-confidence. Believe in yourself and you can achieve great things and help many other people too.

You can choose to fill your life with color and crystal power.

These beautiful treasures from the Earth can help you spiritually, mentally, emotionally, and physically, as well as helping you develop a strong sense of who you are. Crystals, minerals, rocks, metals and gemstones are tools to help you stay focused on your goals and create good things in your life.

How to Use Crystals and Stones

As a young girl, I collected all types of rocks alongside my collection of seashells. I also had the good fortune to have a family friend who introduced me to the magic of believing and the power of positive thought when I was very young. I learned that the power of your imagination and visualization can help you achieve great things. These tools I wish to pass on to you.

Visualization is when you use your imagination to mentally see something even though it is not in front of you. Visualizing is making a mental picture or creating images in your mind.

I call them "tools" because I look at them like tools in a toolbox. The tools include:
- good thoughts.
- looking at things in a positive way.
- pretty crystals, rocks, stones and metals.
- a vivid imagination.
- the ability to visualize.
- the magic of believing that anything is possible.
- the willingness to try, because you won't know if you don't try.

To use the tools from your tool box, start by thinking a positive thought like, "I am smart" or "I can do anything" or "It is easy for me to make friends" or "I am safe and happy". Next, pick up a stone, any stone you like. Hold it in your hand, put it in your pocket or keep it nearby to help you remember to think that good thought. The stone magnifies the thought, making it stronger. Every time you see or touch the stone it will help you maintain your focus on what you *do* want. It will keep you from thinking about what you don't want, or things that you might be afraid of. Keep your attention on the good thought so it replaces any thoughts that are the opposite of what you want. Visualize and make believe that whatever you want already exists. And take the action to make it your *intention*.

An *intention* is a plan, objective or a purpose.

It is important to have an intention and to focus on the positive so that life reflects your highest potential. Everything that is created is created through intention. We create our lives with our thoughts, actions, words and deeds. Our intentions vibrate out into the world and return to us in the form of our personal reality.

When a gemstone is paired with a daily affirmation, the stone amplifies that intention. It is a tool that helps you maintain your focus on what you *do* want. What is your plan? What do you want? Establish your intention.

Activity:

Name three intentions that you would like to have happen:

1. _____

_____

2. _____

_____

3. _____

_____

It is simple to change your mind and change your thoughts. For example, just as you decide you want a glass of water, you start to think about and imagine, visualize, and then take the action to get that glass of water. Anything you want to achieve in your life is no different or more complicated than getting yourself a glass of water. Simply think of the steps you need to take to achieve your goal, then take the action to make it so and you will find it easily happens – it is as simple as getting a glass of water for yourself.

So, how do I pick a stone?

Go to the store or outside in your backyard and just pick one! Don't read about them first, just pick a stone, any stone. You don't need a lot of money to use the tools and techniques offered in this book. The stones within this book are easily found at rock shops or metaphysical stores. If you aren't able to get the stones listed, simply look around in nature to find a stone of a similar color.

> The crystals, minerals and stones listed in this book are those that you can commonly find in metaphysical bookstores and rock shops. The words *crystals, minerals* and *stones* are often used as synonyms throughout the book.

When you go to a store or out into nature to get your stones, start by thinking about what you want to use the stone for (your intention). Do you want the stone to help you with your studies and to get better grades? Or perhaps you want to feel better about yourself? Perhaps you want to feel better about making friends or how your friends and family treat you? You can use a stone to help you with any part of your life. You can use it to help you with your thoughts (mental),

feelings (emotional), body (physical), or your connection with the angels, nature spirits and Spirit (spiritual).

Keep focused on your intention, then start looking at the various choices of stones. You can look at the pictures within this book (*without reading about the stone first*) to see which stone attracts you. You can also go to your local rock shop or metaphysical store to browse through the choices of crystals and stones available.

You will be naturally drawn to what you need. It's best to wait until you have chosen the stones before you look up what the stone is good for. Use the positive thought affirmations in this book with the stone you choose. You can also make up your own affirmations to help you through your day.

So, how do I use the stones?

Using the stones is easy. Simply hold them in your hand and remember your intention. That way you link that intention to the stone(s). Then carry them in your pocket, place them under your pillow at night, place them on your nightstand, use them any way you like, just so that whenever you touch or see that stone you will be reminded of your intention.

Use your imagination, visualize the end result as if your challenge is already better, and remember to stay focused on what you *do* want rather than what you don't want! Ways to use the stones:

- In your hand
- In your pocket
- In your back pack
- In your pillowcase
- Next to your bed
- On your desk
- On your window sill
- Next to your computer
- On the bathroom counter
- Next to the television

There are two Easy Reference Guides at the end of this book. One is by stone name with keywords that relate to issues or problems. The other guide is based on life challenges.

A Little Gemology Lesson

This *very* brief gemology lesson will give you some insight into the names and types of stones.

Rocks are mineral aggregates containing one or more minerals.

Aggregate. Consisting of a mixture of minerals that can be manually separated.

Minerals are naturally-occurring inorganic materials containing chemical, physical, and optical parts.

Crystals are minerals that have smooth sides and have a point and edges.

Gemstone is a broad term that includes both organic materials and man-made inorganic gemlike materials.

Organic. Made up of leaves, roots, and other plant or animal material.
Inorganic. Material composed of minerals, or made from minerals; not animal or vegetable in origin.

Fossils <foss-ills> are the preserved remains of animals, animal parts, plants, and other living organisms from the past.

Quartz <core-ts> is silicon dioxide that crystallizes and is also found in masses. Quartz is found in many forms. Some examples are amethyst, citrine, smoky quartz, rose quartz, and rock crystal quartz, depending on color.

Chalcedony <Cal-said-knee> is a family of stones which includes agate and jasper. They are composed of tiny or microscopic quartz.

Obsidian <ub-sid-ee-an> is a natural glass formed during the cooling of volcanic lava.

There are many ways that rocks grow in the Earth. The most common forms are igneous, metamorphic and sedimentary.

Igneous <ig-knee-us> is a rock that became solid from lava or magma. Magma is liquid rock inside a volcano. Lava is liquid rock (magma) that flows out of a volcano.

Metamorphic <met-a-morf-ik> is a rock that has been changed by heat, pressure, or other natural means.

Sedimentary <said-i-meant-a-ree> *rocks* are types of rock that are formed by the deposit of material at the Earth's surface and within bodies of water.

Gemology is fascinating, isn't it? I'm sure you will learn many exciting geological facts in your physical science books in school. This book is different. This book will provide you with tools to use on a metaphysical level, the level beyond what you can see with your eyes!

Activity:

Have you ever been attracted to a stone?

_____

What kind of stone were you attracted to?

_____

Crystals and the Rainbow Body

Crystals and stones are minerals, meaning they are neither plant nor animal. In other words, they are made up of non-living material. They come in various shapes and sizes. Crystals and stones are also sometimes called gemstones. There are "families" of crystals in which the stones look similar to each other but appear in various colors and slightly different shapes and sizes.

Crystals come in a rainbow of colors. These colors indicate how you can use the stone to help you in your life. You are also made up of many colors. *Everyone* has a rainbow body. We are all beings of light composed of seven main **chakras**, or energy centers, and each has a color.

The energy centers of the body (the chakras) are bands of energy holding the mental, physical, spiritual and emotional bodies of your awareness. The four bodies, both visible and invisible, create the aura or energy which surrounds your body. The mental body is the part of you that thinks. The emotional body is the part of you that feels, the spiritual body is the part of you connected with the Universal Life Force or God, and the physical body is the place where your soul and spirit live here on Earth. It is good to understand that there are four levels of awareness within every aspect of your life. It helps you know why you feel, think, act or react in certain ways in various situations.

Each of these energy centers has a color associated with it, and together these colors make up the rainbow body. The many colorful crystals and stones can help us to understand and deal with challenging situations as they relate to each of these energy centers. Each of these energy centers has a lot of information stored inside that can help you understand yourself, and your friends and family.

Life doesn't happen to us; we create it with our thoughts, actions, words and deeds. A simple desire to be happy and loved forms an intention. With a little bit of know-how, any of us can change an intention or thought into reality. We all make choices and develop beliefs through the stories we tell ourselves.

As we become aware of our choices, we have the ability to improve how we relate with others. Being aware of your choices can help you feel better about yourself and raise your self-confidence. This can help you in how you get along with your friends and your family. As you get to understand your thoughts and feelings better even your schoolwork can improve because you'll learn how to stay focused on the lesson.

Because each energy center or chakra is a specific color, you can use gemstones of a specific color to help you with that energy center. The stone is simply a tool or a reminder of what you want to achieve.

Let's say you need to present a paper or report at school and you are feeling a bit nervous or shy about standing up and talking in front of your classmates. There are stones that help with self-confidence. One of them is citrine. You can hold the citrine <sit-treen> when you practice your report. You can put the citrine in your pillowcase every night before you fall asleep. You can put the citrine in your pocket when you give your report. Because of the color and the qualities already within the stone, it can help you be self-confident while you give the report.

It's not the stone that gives you the confidence; it is your plan to be self-confident that does the trick. The citrine is the reminder that keeps you focused on your goal. Put your goal into the stone by gazing at it and remembering that every time you touch it, look at it, or think of it, it will help you refocus your attention and awareness on your goal, thereby bringing you a step closer to your plan.

It takes focus and grounding to keep your attention on your goal. Notice I used the word "grounding". The word "grounding" or "grounded" used throughout this book means being centered, focused, and determined to block out distractions. It means getting back to earth vs. being spaced out. Please don't confuse it with being grounded because you got into trouble!

Mother Earth has provided these gemstone tools in all the colors of the rainbow and in every shape imaginable. Each of the gemstones relates directly to one of your chakras or energy centers. To determine which gemstone you should use, it is best to be aware of the colors that are associated with each of the chakras (see illustration) as well as the meaning and purpose of each chakra (discussed in the chapters to follow). With this basic information, you can then use gemstones in your daily life.

Each chapter to follow includes a discussion of crystal/gemstones and how they relate to particular energy centers, and provides affirmations for use with the crystals. Affirmations are positive thoughts. Think good thoughts while you hold your stones and good things will come to you. Gemstones, such as agate, quartz, tourmaline, calcite,

and jasper, come in a variety of colors and will therefore appear under more than one color energy or chakra. Although the actual minerals hold specific vibrations, the color of the stone is a more important consideration in combination with the area of your life you are working on.

Every time you see or touch a stone, you reactivate your goal and focus on your plan. Repeat the positive thought affirmation in your heart and mind. Let the crystals and gemstones shine their light and add the full spectrum of color to light up your life with joy, happiness, self-confidence and laughter!

THE CHAKRAS AND ASSOCIATED COLORS

7	Crown: The top of the head	Violet
6	Third Eye: The middle of the forehead	Indigo
5	Throat: The area around the neck	Pastel or Turquoise Blue
4	Heart: The center of the chest	Green and Pink
3	Solar Plexus: Just above the belly button	Yellow
2	Belly: Just below your belly button	Orange
1	Root: The base of the spine	Red

Everyone is a living, breathing rainbow of sound, color, and vibration!

1.
Red Energy

Physical energy, earth connection, survival needs

Chakra: root

Colors: black, brown, metallic gray, red

Stones: agate, black tourmaline, garnet, hematite, jasper

Other stones for balance: chrysocolla, green aventurine, sodalite

Keywords: grounding, health, money, nutrition, protection, safety

Just as a tree has roots deep in the Earth to keep it firmly planted, so are the roots of your own thoughts and beliefs stored within the root chakra at the base of your spine. This chakra is all about the physical part of your life which includes a safe place to live, healthy food to eat, and good water to drink. The root chakra is also the part of you that learns to earn money and save money as well as how to spend it wisely.

How does red energy feel?
Red energy is the energy for LIFE. The Earth is filled with red energy.

Imagine you are a tree, and you have roots that go down deep into the Earth. Now imagine pulling that red energy up from the Earth, through your roots and into your body. That warm feeling is red energy!

The color red and red stones help you have energy and strength. Red energy connects you to the Earth and nurtures your whole body.

Red energy in balance
You feel safe and self-confident (at least *most* of the time), and you are able to concentrate in class and on your homework.

Too little red energy
You might feel tired even though you've had enough sleep, or you might feel alone or cut-off. Maybe you feel unsure of yourself, or others are pushing you around?

> *Keep a hematite or black tourmaline in your pocket or back pack and imagine that the stones are creating a force field of protection so that bullies can't bother you. Imagine some blue and green colors to calm you.*

Use stones like black tourmaline, garnet, hematite, red jasper.

Too much red energy
You might be too intense or aggressive without meaning to be.

> *Imagine recycling extra red energy by sending it out of your feet, back down your roots and into the Earth.*

Use green and blue stones for balance like chrysocolla, green aventurine or sodalite.

Balanced red energy helps you ...
- stay grounded.
- feel safe and secure.
- get motivated.
- stay focused.

- dance, run, create and play.
- release feelings of anger and frustration.

In addition to the red rocks in this chapter, many of the stones listed here are brown, black, or metallic gray as well. All the stones listed in this chapter, regardless of color, are for the root chakra. These are the stones to help you if you are looking out the window or around your classroom at others instead of staying focused on your paper or work. These stones are good study buddies. Choose a rock you like and make it your study stone.

The metallic gray, brown and black stones are helpful for those with symptoms appearing like ADD, ADHD or autism. It is an alternative therapy to help you feel safe and focused.

The root chakra stones – red, black, brown, grey and metallic – can help you feel comfortable and protected. You can put a stone in your pillowcase or in your hand when you go to bed if you are afraid of the dark. Hold the stone, say some prayers, and think good thoughts and you'll fall asleep peacefully.

Agate <a-gat>

Agate comes in many colors. Regardless of the color, agate gemstones are grounding.

Agate can be used with any chakra, according to color. In the case of the root chakra, red, brown, black and gray agates are good. A brown or black agate is grounding. It helps you stay centered and calm. An orange agate can get you moving.

Agate Positive Thought Affirmation: I am grounded and focused. I now finish all my homework. I get all my chores done easily and enjoy doing them too!

Black Tourmaline <tur-ma-lean>

Black tourmaline keeps away the bad stuff! It wards off negativity, and puts up a force field so anything scary or uncomfortable can't enter your space, and helps you remember you are safe.

Black tourmaline helps reduce the effects of electromagnetic frequencies (EMFs) or harmful waves coming from cell phones and computers. Even the remote control for your TV and cable box releases these frequencies. Place black tourmaline by your TV, computer, cell phone or other electronic device to lessen the effects of EMFs.

Black tourmaline helps keep you centered. It helps you refocus if you seem to be easily distracted. If you have a habit of looking around the classroom instead of focusing on your work or what is being taught in the classroom, carry or wear black tourmaline until you re-train and re-balance your energy fields. Every time you touch or see the stone, remind yourself to stay focused on the task or assignment at hand. With practice, you can do it!

Black Tourmaline Positive Thought Affirmation: I am protected. All negative energy bounces off me. I have a force field of love and well-being around me. I am grounded, centered, and able to maintain focus on the task at hand.

Garnet <gar-net>

Do you put things off for another day? Do you have an assignment that you really need to finish? Garnet is a great stone to get you moving and motivated if you feel lazy or put things off. It can also help you get fresh ideas and then follow through. It is one thing to think of a good idea and it's another thing to take action and make it happen! With garnet nearby, you can get focused on a project of any kind. Whether it is your homework, your chores around the house or something a bit more fun like art or music, use the positive thought below to help you achieve your goal.

Garnet Positive Thought Affirmation: I am grounded and focused. I am very creative. I follow through with my thoughts and ideas. It's easy for me to get moving and make things happen!

Hematite <heem-a-tight>

Hematite helps you calm and focus yourself. This metallic gray stone is good for someone with a tendency to be scattered and easily distracted. Hematite is helpful if you are hyperactive and want to calm down, stay focused and do one thing at a time. It calms hyperactivity.

Create a grid of hematite and rose quartz in your bedroom to help with good study habits and good sleep. To create a grid place stones around your room to create a force field of good thoughts. For example, place hematite under the four corners of the mattress and rose quartz around the room. If your room is where you study, then be sure to place the hematite on your desk as well.

Hematite combined with rose quartz helps release fears when you feel unsafe or in need of protection, and fills you with loving energy. See page 32 for a fun activity using hematite and rose quartz.

Hematite Positive Thought Affirmation: I am calm and relaxed. My muscles are relaxed. Everything is okay now and will be okay in the future. There is nothing to worry about. All is well.

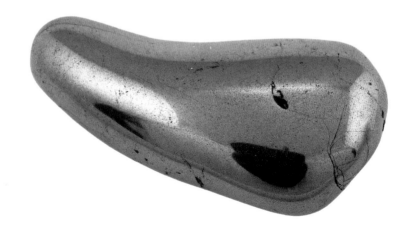

Jasper <Jass-pur>

Jasper occurs in shades of red, brown, orange and yellow. Jaspers come variegated, picturesque and mottled. *Variegated* means it has markings of various colors. *Picturesque* means it looks painted or has a painted scene on it. *Mottled* means it has colored spots on it like the dalmatian jasper shown below. Jasper is grounding and helps you maintain focus. It is also a stone of protection, motivation and creativity. Creativity can mean having fun creating stories, art, songs, dances, or making a show with your friends to entertain family and neighbors.

Red jasper stimulates creativity. Take action as you use red jasper, keeping your positive thought in mind. The dalmatian jasper is mostly white with black spots just like the Dalmatian dog. It brings out loyalty and balance.

Red Jasper Positive Thought Affirmation: I am grounded and focused. I am motivated to get up and accomplish all that needs to be done.

Dalmatian Jasper Positive Thought Affirmation: I am in balance. I am grateful for all my loyal friends and family. I am a good and loyal friend.

Obsidian <obb-sid-ee-in>

Obsidian is volcanic glass that naturally occurs in igneous rocks. Igneous rocks are stones that solidified from lava or magma. It has been used to make arrowheads, spear tips and other tools by various cultures including the Stone Age, pre-Columbian (before the arrival of Columbus in America), Mesoamerican and Native American cultures. The most common colors are black and brown.

You can find black obsidian in tumbled form, arrowheads, and nodules called apache tears. All black obsidian helps in setting up a protective vibration. There is a reflective quality in all forms of obsidian because it is glass and acts like a mirror. The incoming energies bounce off, like light off of a mirror, and therefore protect you and your belongings.

Apache tears are beneficial when you are sad or grieving the loss of a pet or loved one. Apache tears can be used to balance the emotions, yet they promote healthy crying to release the sadness of the loss.

There are variations of black obsidian:

- Snowflake obsidian has white snowflake-like markings reminding you that there is always light within the darkness.
- Rainbow obsidian has colors streaming throughout it. This stone is a perfect representation of black containing all the colors of the rainbow. At first glance, it is dense and dark, but the rainbow is reflecting deep inside. Even though you cannot see the chakra system and the rainbow body, they still exist. Rainbow obsidian is a tool for remembering all that you are.
- The golden sheen in golden sheen obsidian is formed from little bubbles that occur during the cooling process of the lava flow. The sheen within black obsidian offers an additional reflective quality to deflect negativity. It is good for protection, and is helpful if you are around people who argue a lot to help you feel less upset.

You can hold onto obsidian when you argue with your brothers, sisters or friends over sharing your toys and belongings. It is also helpful if you or your classmates are bickering over rules of a game, or anything at all.

Rainbow Obsidian Positive Thought Affirmation: I remember I have all the colors in my rainbow body. The colors are aligned and balanced. I remember that there is a full spectrum of light – a rainbow – even when everything appears to be dark or challenging.

Snowflake Obsidian Positive Thought Affirmation: I am able to see the good in all things. I can imagine good things even when things seem too hard to handle. I know there is always hope. I trust I can get help to pull me through when I am afraid.

Golden Sheen Obsidian Positive Thought Affirmation: I create my own reality. I think good thoughts. My imagination makes up good and happy things and then they become true. My thoughts become things. I am safe. There is only goodness, love and well-being in my life.

Black Obsidian Apache Tear Positive Thought Affirmation: I am safe. I easily drive away anything that is scary. I find the good within. I am protected. My friends and I get along well together. Even when my friends and I have differences, we are still friends. All is well.

Activity:

Visualize yourself inside a pink crystal ball, rose quartz. Imagine that the outside of the rose quartz crystal ball has a layer of hematite. Know that the hematite pushes away anything scary or uncomfortable and the rose quartz increases feelings of safety and happiness.

How did you feel after doing this visualization activity?

_____

_____

_____

2.
Orange Energy

Energy, self-motivation, creativity

Chakra: belly, also known as navel or sacral

Colors: orange, peach

Stones: Carnelian, orange calcite, tiger's eye

Other stones for balance: chrysocolla, malachite

Keywords: action, creativity, emotions, feelings

The belly chakra, also known as the navel or sacral chakra, is the energy center that holds the vibration of creativity and fertility. It is the place of having the courage to take action to create the life you want. The orange of this chakra is the part of the chakra system associated with creativity. Your creation might be a beautiful piece of art, a great presentation for a school project, an attractive outfit, or the décor of your room. The orange vibe adds energy to the creative process, as well as promoting the action necessary to make these artistic actions happen.

You have the power to be and do anything. It is up to you what you wish to have or to be. Feel the orange energy and step into action!

How does orange energy feel?

Orange energy is CREATIVITY and ENERGY. You always have great ideas and the ability to achieve your goals.

Imagine you have the color orange swirling around you. In the swirls are ideas, pictures, and the ability to create them. Now imagine you are taking those ideas and taking action to build, to draw, to make them real.

The color orange and orange stones help you bring ideas and visions into reality. Orange connects you to your natural ability to create.

Orange energy in balance

You feel energized with great ideas. You feel joyful. You have a great imagination and you are able to take the ideas from your imagination and use them. You can invent, draw, and create easily. It is easy for you to finish what you start.

Too little orange energy

You might feel lazy. Maybe you don't feel like doing your chores or your homework. You might feel bored and tired. You procrastinate and find that your parents, teachers or friends have to keep reminding you to get things done. It seems you don't finish what you start.

Keep an orange calcite or carnelian on your desk and write down all that you need to do. Place the stone near your "to do" list and tackle one chore at a time. Check things off your list as you finish them to help you see all you have accomplished. Place an orange stone in your pocket and imagine that it is giving you the energy you need to want to get everything done.

Use stones like carnelian, orange calcite, and tiger's eye.

Too much orange energy

You might be too emotional and hyper-active without meaning to be. You might feel like crying.

> *Imagine the colors blue and green flowing around you. Place a chrysocolla or malachite in your hand. Connect with the feelings you are having and imagine that you can put those feelings inside the stone in your hand. Now look at the stone and look at those feelings like you are watching a movie. See how your feel when you complete this visualization.*

Use other stones for balance like chrysocolla and malachite.

Balanced orange energy helps you ...

- be friendly and kind with others.
- be optimistic and a positive thinker.
- have a sense of belonging and the confidence to include yourself and be included in groups.
- be creative and have the ability to create stories, songs, dances and more.
- follow your gut intuition, using your feelings and senses to guide you through life.
- finish projects and homework easily.
- have the ability to deal with negative emotions and feelings.

In addition to the orange stones in this chapter, I have also listed a blue-green stone. Chrysocolla and other blue or green stones help you calm uncomfortable feelings and overly dramatic emotional reactions. Hold onto the blue or green stones when you need to calm down. While a good cry is good for you once in a while, too much emotional unrest is very tiring.

You can put a stone in your pillowcase or in your hand when you feel too emotional or can't stop crying. Hold the stone, say some prayers, and think good thoughts and you'll start to feel better. Try wearing blue or green clothes on days when you are feeling emotionally upset and notice how much better you feel.

Calcite <cal-sight>

Calcite occurs in orange, blue, honey, brown, green, pink, red and clear. Orange calcite as well as honey calcite is good for the belly chakra. Calcite appears in different forms like masses or chunks, rhomboid and dogtooth formations. Dogtooth calcite is the gemstone found in crystal caves forming stalactites and stalagmites.

Orange calcite helps calm muscle spasms, relax back pain and restore balance to ligaments and tendons. After all, it is your muscles, back and ligaments that support your physical body. If you want extra help with gym class (also known as P.E. or physical education) or anything athletic, use orange calcite with a positive thought affirmation. Use the positive thought with the stone in your pocket or nearby when planning tennis, basketball, bowling, softball, or any type of sport.

Orange calcite realigns the emotions. Calcite can assist you when you're going through change. Change is the only thing that is constant in life. Calcite helps shift the anxiety associated with change. That anxiety is simply the fear of the unknown. Although calcite is a stone, there is a sort of softness about it.

Calcite comes in many colors and all colors of calcite help during life transitions or changes. Calcite is comforting when parents get divorced. Or use calcite as a buddy when you have to attend a new school, make new friends, and get adjusted in a new home. Calcite helps you with anything that is new or different because, at first, change can feel uncomfortable.

Orange calcite is a good stone to help you bring your creative ideas to life. Use it when you are working on an art project or developing a piece of music. It will add courage to your very fine inspiration.

Orange Calcite Positive Thought Affirmation: Change is good. I easily shift into this next part of my life. I easily visualize and imagine good things in my life. I have balanced emotions. My bones and muscles are strong and I feel good in my body. I am physically fit.

Carnelian <car-neal-yun>

Carnelian is a stone that helps you to create and take action in your life. It helps you to bring your creative ideas into reality. Carnelian helps you feel the courage to both start and finish creative projects.

It can also help balance feelings of anger or frustration and turn them into feelings of courage and joy through your creative projects. Hold a piece of carnelian as you take a deep breath and visualize your lungs filling up with air completely. The distraction of focusing on your breathing can push away anger and frustration.

Put a carnelian in your pocket while working on a piece of art, an essay or story, or composing music. The creative vibe of carnelian will help you take the action necessary to complete the task.

Carnelian Positive Thought Affirmation: I breathe easily and know that all is well. I take in a deep breath of life and breathe out in a relaxed, even flow. I release all anger in a healthy, balanced way. I am creative. I move forward and take action on the things that need to be accomplished.

Chrysocolla <kris-a-cola>

What is a blue-green stone doing in the orange energy section? Although chrysocolla is a blue-green stone, it is good for balancing the energy at the belly chakra because it is the complimentary color to orange on the color wheel. Sometimes the opposite color for a given energy center can bring balance and alignment. The colors of blue and green have a calming effect. Too much orange can make you anxious or frustrated. Add blue or green colored stones to help take away those negative feelings.

Chrysocolla can be used at any chakra for balance, calm, and inner peace. Chrysocolla contains azurite, malachite and cuprite. Together they create a team of minerals to calm jittery feelings, frustration, aggravation and muscular inflammations.

You can use good thoughts as a tool to heal abuse and anger. Chrysocolla is the stone to turn to when you are dealing with the more difficult issues, emotions or feelings. Grab chrysocolla and sit with a journal or notebook. Let yourself write out what needs to be worked through and watch how much better you feel after you get

your feelings or concerns out of you and onto the paper. Keep a chrysocolla in your pocket when you are feeling hurt by the anger of someone else.

Chrysocolla Positive Thought Affirmation: I am calm and at peace. I am able to accept myself, my feelings and my emotions. I release uncomfortable feelings to heal anger. I am safe. I allow the nurturing vibrations of Mother Earth to surround me.

Tiger's Eye

Tiger's eye has a luminous, reflective effect like a sheen or a shimmer. The most common colors of tiger's eye are golden brown and red. The reflective quality is what contributes to its ability to repel or keep away negativity. Tiger's eye can be used to remove negative thoughts regardless of whether those thoughts are yours or belong to someone else. This stone is often used as an amulet to remove or keep away jealousy or any type of negative vibes. An amulet is an object intended to bring about good luck or protection.

Use the red tiger's eye to motivate you to take the required action to finish projects, tasks or homework. You can use it to instill high

self-esteem and courage. Red tiger's eye can also be used at the root chakra level for red energy.

Gold Tiger's Eye Positive Thought Affirmation: I am safe. I am confident. I am aligned with my personal power. I set boundaries easily. Goodness surrounds me wherever I go and whatever I do!

Red Tiger's Eye Positive Thought Affirmation: I have a lot of energy. I am self-motivated. I am strong and courageous.

Activity:

Gather paper and colored pencils, crayons, paint, or markers. Draw what you feel inside. What colors did you choose? As you continue to read through this book, look at your drawing to note the meaning of the colors.

Self-confidence, mental clarity, happiness.
Be all that you can be!

Chakra: solar plexus

Colors: yellow, green, purple

Stones: amber, amethyst, apatite, citrine, goldstone, jasper

Other stones for balance: malachite, peridot

Keywords: self-confidence, mental clarity, happiness, courage

Self-confidence and self-esteem are the keys to this energy center. The main color of the solar plexus is yellow. It is located just above your belly button. This is the center that stores the energy to live your life with confidence and courage. It is the place where you remember that you are fantastic and you can be and do anything!

How does yellow energy feel?
Yellow energy is HAPPY and JOYFUL. You feel good about yourself and you have the courage to stand up for yourself.

Imagine you have the sun shining brightly from your solar plexus. In the rays of light that stream forth from your yellow energy center, feel the warmth vibrating from you like a powerful force.

In the rays of yellow light are all your positive qualities. You can do anything!

The color yellow and yellow stones help you see the good in everything – in yourself and in others. It connects you to happiness and feeling good about yourself.

Yellow energy in balance

You believe and know you can do anything you put your mind to. You feel joyful. You see things in a positive light. You can integrate and absorb all that life has to offer. It is easy for you to think clearly, laugh easily, and be happy for yourself and others. It is easy to stand up for yourself and keep others from pushing you around.

Too little yellow energy

You might lack confidence or feel embarrassed or self-conscious. Maybe you feel left out or worry your friends don't like you. You could find that you are jealous of your friends or school mates. You might let others push you around or bully you. You might be confused or have a hard time staying focused on your studies or projects.

Keep amber, citrine, or peridot in your pocket or school bag. Think about all the reasons you feel the way you do. Place the stone near you and imagine you have the yellow energy from the citrine and amber shining brightly around you with a bit of green to keep away jealous or negative feelings. Remind yourself that you are amazing and deserve the best.

Use stones like amber, amethyst, citrine and peridot.

Too much yellow energy

You are probably thinking too much. Perhaps you are worrying about things, which can make you feel even worse. You might be thinking about things that haven't even happened or aren't even real or true.

Imagine the colors green and purple flowing around you. Place a malachite or amethyst in your hand. Bring to mind the thoughts that are bothering you, and imagine putting them inside a purple balloon. Now imagine the balloon carrying those thoughts far far away, never to return. Now connect with the stone(s) and tell yourself that every time you think of the stone or look at the stone you are replacing the worrying thought with positive thoughts.

Use other stones for balance like peridot and malachite.

Balanced yellow energy helps you …

- increase your self-confidence and good feelings about yourself.
- find courage and self-esteem when feeling shy.
- digest food easily, including sugars and foods that can cause sensitivities.
- establish healthy boundaries, including speaking up if something is inappropriate or if you feel uncomfortable because of another person's actions or words.
- achieve anything you put your mind to.
- feel happy and joyful.
- think clearly and share your intelligence.

Imagine the sun shining at your solar plexus, warming you up and helping you to receive all that life has to offer. You are worthy of all that is good!

In addition to the yellow stones in this chapter, some are green and one is even purple. Purple is the opposite color to yellow on the color wheel. Regardless of color, all the stones listed here can help with the challenges or qualities of the solar plexus energy center, which is located just above your belly button and just below the center of your chest.

If you are feeling insecure, you can put a stone in your hand and daydream about how special you are. Hold the stone, say some prayers, think good thoughts and make up a little story that helps you remember how special you are. Be creative. Do something to make yourself happy today!

Amber <am-bur>

Amber is petrified pine resin. It holds the ancient wisdom of the trees. According to ancient legends and folklore, trees provide profound spiritual wisdom.

Amber is good for setting boundaries and trusting your feelings. Hold onto the vision of being respected and treated well by your friends, as well as all groups and cliques. Use amber to maintain your own energy field and keep other people's energy fields distinctly separate from yours, in a loving way.

Amber Positive Thought Affirmation: I easily set boundaries with others. I surround myself with people who respect me, my things, and my space. I am protected from the thoughts and feelings of others. I feel nurtured and cared for.

Amethyst

Amethyst is great for changing any situation. Use it when you are having trouble with friends, or any situation where you feel you don't have the ability to change the outcome.

I remember once I took a trip through Italy and Germany with two girls whom I considered friends. I was feeling exceptionally vulnerable at the time because my mom had passed away that year. As the days went by, the two girls were mean to me in their actions and words. Even though I was an adult, I felt like I was being bullied by people I thought were my friends. It made me lose some self-confidence for a day or two. But not for long! I put on my amethyst necklace and imagined I was inside a cocoon of purple light. Anytime they said or did anything mean, I imagined that the swirling purple energy of the

color and the amethyst necklace was transforming and transmuting it so that it couldn't affect me. It worked! Within a few days they changed their attitude and moved on to do other things. I was free of their negativity and enjoyed my trip.

Amethyst and citrine also occur in the same stone. This heart-shaped stone is called ametrine. It is ideal for transforming negativity and increasing your self-confidence.

Amethyst or Ametrine Positive Thought Affirmation: I see, sense, feel and know that life is magical. It is easy for me to change things for the better by imagining a better way. I am blessed to have only goodness and love around me.

Apatite <app-a-tight>

This stone is good when you have stomachache. Just as the name of the stone sounds, it is the stone for balancing your appetite and maintaining the right weight. If you are too slender and have a hard time keeping weight on, it will bring balance. If you are overweight, it will assist you in bringing balance. The focus isn't so much on gaining weight and losing weight as much as it is on creating balance, health and well-being. When used with positive thoughts, apatite can aid in the proper absorption of nutrients, and the digestion of food within the body.

Apatite works on all levels. The ability to manifest your desires in the world requires that you understand your feelings, deep down in your soul. Apatite helps you focus on maintaining a good diet, but on another level it helps you understand what is going on around you. Therefore, before going on an eating plan to gain or lose weight, take a look at how you are digesting life and how you feel about it.

Are you able to metaphorically swallow and take in all that is happening in your world? Is it too much for you to handle? Do you feel deprived in some way? The awareness must take place mentally, emotionally and spiritually. Once you become aware of your feelings, thoughts and emotions, true and complete healing can take place.

Apatite Positive Thought Affirmation: I digest my food with ease. I easily digest life. My appetite is balanced and healthy. My body maintains the perfect weight. The people in my life are supportive and calming.

Citrine <sit-reen>

Do you know you are magnificent? It is time to remember and embrace your magnificence! You are a shining star. Use the golden ray of citrine to boost your self-esteem and self-confidence. Citrine helps you to shine your light brightly and be all that you can be, with joy and courage. It helps you feel secure enough to speak up for yourself. Citrine also provides the brilliance to bring mental clarity and clear insight. Do you know you create your own reality? Use this stone of manifestation to help you create your reality. It also helps with clearing mental blocks for writers and artists.

Citrine Positive Thought Affirmation: I am courageous and shine my light brightly. I am very good at setting boundaries. I am confident and realize that people honor and respect me. I am a valued person in society. I am mentally clear.

Activity:

Name 3 things that make you magnificent.

1. _____

2. _____

3. _____

Hold a citrine in your hand and come up with 3 more things.

1. _____

2. _____

3. _____

Goldstone

Goldstone is actually a man-made stone and isn't really a stone at all; it is glass made from copper and copper salts. It was first made in the 17th Century by a family in Venice, although folklore maintains it was made by Italian monks. It has been referred to as "monk's gold" even though the origins of the folklore can't be found. This coppery-gold vibration has a natural resonance to wealth, abundance and prosperity.

There is a starry quality to the goldstone which brings inner reflection as well as a reminder that you are a shining star. Gazing into goldstone reminds you of all you can be, and to shine your many talents brightly.

Goldstone in any color provides support for your self-esteem and the solar plexus. Goldstone comes in red, blue and green. The orangey red vibration is grounding, while also activating courage and passion for life. It is beneficial for the navel as well as for the solar plexus.

Red Goldstone Positive Thought Affirmation: I shine my light brightly and sparkle for all to see. I shine my light as I live fully and passionately. I am a shining star! I am focused and aligned. I have balanced emotions.

Jasper <Jass-pur>

Yellow jasper is good for grounding and helps you maintain focus. It is one of the stones of protection. Use the yellow variety for increasing the feeling that it is safe to shine your light brightly, and to have the courage to be all that you can be in a down-to-earth way. Yellow jasper brings forth the gut feeling of knowing you are safe, protected and free to be you.

Yellow Jasper Positive Thought Affirmation: It is safe to be myself. My self-confidence gives me the courage to be all I can be. It is easy for me to achieve my goals. It is safe to be powerful, in a loving way.

Malachite <mal-a-kite>

Yes, there is a green stone in the yellow energy section! You can use malachite as a solar plexus stone and as a heart chakra stone, too. You'll read more about malachite in the next chapter. Malachite is helpful for digestion – by holding it and using the positive thought affirmation. *Caution! Do not put this stone or any other stones in water that you drink, or ingest the stone in any way.* It's the *energy* of the stone that you are using, along with your positive thought.

Malachite assists in the ability to take in the sweetness of life because it is also a heart chakra stone. It also offers pancreatic support for people with diabetes, therefore it helps with digesting sugar. Use malachite to release the vibration of diabetes from your energy field. Focus on sending messages of health, love and well-being to your liver and pancreas as you follow your doctor's instructions.

Malachite Positive Thought Affirmation: I digest all I take in, easily, and receive all the benefits. My heart is focused on love, light and well-being. Even when things appear to be swirling around me, I am able to stay focused. I am able to process and digest all the sweetness life offers me on all levels.

Peridot < perry -doe>

Peridot is a green stone also known as olivine. This gem has been identified in meteorites and on the Moon and Mars. Peridot helps you look at things in a different way.

Peridot is good for the wounded healer. In native and indigenous cultures, the wounded healer is someone who has overcome their illness through natural or non-traditional means and now provides those insights to help others.

Peridot is helpful for digestion on all levels. The green color resembles the color of bile, which is a digestive fluid. Peridot helps with anger and jealousy. Peridot is good for the person who is feeling jealous or angry, and also the person to whom the anger or jealousy is directed.

Peridot Positive Thought Affirmation: I ward off jealousy. I keep away people who are jealous and attract people who are happy for me. I have a healthy digestive system. I am able to digest life and all that it brings my way with ease and grace.

Tiger's Eye

Tiger's eye has a luminous, reflective quality with a sheen or a shimmer. The most common color of tiger's eye is golden brown. The reflective quality is what contributes to its ability to deflect or repel negativity. Use tiger's eye to keep away negative thoughts. This stone has been known historically to ward off the evil eye.

If you have a tendency toward secretly being jealous of someone else's good fortune, hold tight to your tiger's eye and use it to help you figure out what you can do in your life to create similar health, wealth, joy, happiness, friendship, instead of using your time being jealous. Raise your self-esteem and take action to create your life as you wish it to be! Golden brown tiger's eye is an excellent stone for improving your self-esteem, mental clarity and creativity.

Golden Brown Tiger's Eye Affirmation: I am safe. I have constant protection surrounding me, deflecting anything that is not for my highest good. I am grateful I have the courage and self-confidence to create my world.

Activity:

Do you ever feel jealous or have low self-esteem?

Which yellow energy stone do you think will help you feel safe and confident? Look at the photos of the gemstones or your own collection of stones and pick one or two.

Apatite

Amethyst

Citrine

Amber

Goldstone

Jasper

Malachite

Peridot

Tiger's Eye

4.
Green and Pink Energy

Love, compassion, kindness, friendships

Chakra: heart

Colors: green, pink

Stones: chrysoprase, green goldstone, green calcite, malachite, pink calcite, rhodochrosite, rose quartz, unakite

Other stones for balance: same as above

Keywords: love, compassion, kindness, friendship, comfort

You are love. All that you are and all that you do, say, think, feel, smell, taste, or know is love. Remember that truth and you will be happy and healthy all of your life. The green and pink energy of the heart chakra is located in the center of your chest. The primary color is green yet pink is also important for this energy center. Take a bit of the red of the base chakra, and white from the crown that you'll soon be reading about, and blend them together. What do you get when you blend red and white? Pink!

How does green and pink energy feel?

Green is the color of NATURE and pink is the energy of KINDNESS, NURTURING and LOVE. When you feel green and pink energy you feel good, loved, happy, and full of kindness.

Imagine you have the colors green and pink swirling around you. In the swirls are people you love and those who love you. There is also the energy of good friends and nature. Now imagine you are allowing all those good feelings to surround you like your favorite blanket and pillow. You are loved!

The colors green and pink, as well as green and pink stones, help you remember the love that you are, and they help you to always be kind to others.

Green and pink energy in balance

You feel a sense of belonging. You are happy. You have loving family and good friends. You have the ability to see the good in people and situations. You laugh often and feel very joyful!

Too little green and pink energy

You might feel unloved. Maybe you feel your friends aren't being nice to you. You might feel unhappy or that you can't see the good in life. You might need more hugs and reassurance. You probably want attention from those closest to you.

Keep stones like pink calcite, rose quartz or green aventurine in your pillow case. Every night as you fall asleep, use your imagination to make up a story about how nice people are to you! Imagine them showing their love to you through kind actions and including you in all their parties or playtime. When you wake up in the morning, before you get out of bed, take a moment to think of all the people who love and appreciate you. Send them some pink and green energy. Imagine it swirling right back to you and know that it surrounds you all day long!

Other stones you can use are pink-dyed agate, green-dyed agate, green calcite, chrysoprase and unakite.

Too much pink and green energy

You can never have too much pink and green energy. Pink and green energy is LOVE!

Imagine the pink and green surrounding you always.
Remember – you are love! You are loved!

Balanced pink and green energy helps you …

- feel happy and joyful.
- feel loved and loving.
- have good friendships.
- have a good relationship with yourself.
- relate well with your family.
- feel and show compassion, kindness, empathy and understanding.
- see the good in all things.
- accept others and yourself.

Imagine beautiful green light and pink light streaming out from the center of your chest. To get your imagination flowing, visualize yourself walking in green-filled nature with a pink cotton candy in your hand.

There are no opposite colors for the pink and green energy of your heart. Use all pink and green stones to increase feelings of being loved. Hold some rose quartz when you need more attention or some hugs when no one is available to provide them. As you hold the stone, imagine being hugged and remember – you are LOVE!

You can put a pink or green stone, like unakite or pink dyed-agate, in your pocket or in a little pouch in your school bag. Even thinking of the stones can help you focus on feeling loved. Use pink and green energy when you realize you aren't being nice to your friends or family. Hold the stone and make a promise to yourself to be nice. Think good thoughts until you readjust to being the sweet and kind person you truly are. Try wearing pink and green clothes on days when you need to be nicer to others or when you want others to be nicer to you.

Agate

This gemstone comes in many colors. Many of the brighter agate stones like the bright green, hot pink, dark blue and vibrant purple are dyed. These dyes in no way detract or take away from the good vibes of the stones. Agate stones also come in multi-colored slices. Slices are pretty to place in a stand on a windowsill – let the light shine through it, let the light shine on the good vibrations! Both green- and pink-dyed agate open your heart.

Use pink-dyed agate or green-dyed agate to help you get along with others and make friends. It is also good to help you keep loyal friends. Pink- and green-dyed agate stones are good to use when you want to feel loved.

Green-dyed or Pink-dyed Agate Positive Thought Affirmation: I allow love. My heart is open. It's easy for me to make and keep good friends.

Calcite <cal-sight>

Pink and green calcite supports you during a change of heart. Calcite is very nurturing for your heart center during a change in relationship, such as a change in friendships or a divorce in a family. Use pink or green calcite when you need to give yourself permission to change. It is OK to change. It is safe for life to change and it is safe for relationships to change. Love is always available to you even when change is happening.

Pink or Green Calcite Positive Thought Affirmation: I feel nurtured by my friends and family. I am blessed with nurturing vibrations wherever I go! I am gentle. All change brings more love and better life situations.

Chrysoprase <kris-o-praise>

The soothing green semi-opaque or transparent color of this stone brings peace and calm to your heart. It is a heart chakra stone and provides the peace of the ocean waves gently lapping at the shore. Chrysoprase, a member of the chalcedony <kal-said-knee> family of stones, is an apple green or a sea foam green color.

Because of the soothing energy of the green shades of chrysoprase, you may use it to make you feel better when you are sad or heart-broken. It's a helpful reminder that you are loved.

Chrysoprase Positive Thought Affirmation: All is well. Everything is OK. My heart is open and I allow love. I am nurtured. I am nurturing.

Goldstone

As mentioned earlier, goldstone is actually a man-made glass. It really isn't a stone but glass made from copper and copper salts. It can still help you increase good intention, especially when you stay focused on what you want. Green goldstone activates your heart and opens it to give and receive love.

Green Goldstone Positive Thought Affirmation: I open my heart and shine the love that I am to all with whom I come into contact. I have plenty of money. I am blessed with the greatest family and wonderful friends.

Green Aventurine

This green stone is the shamrock of the gemstone kingdom. It carries the vibration of good luck and good fortune. It's great for travel and you can use it with good intention to have a fun, safe, smooth journey. Green aventurine is a tool like all the stones and can be used to activate good luck and remind you that you are a lucky person.

Likewise, employ green aventurine to bring more prosperity – green money! Keep it wherever you keep your money: your wallet, pocket, piggy bank, or secret hiding place.

Green Aventurine Positive Thought Affirmation: I am so grateful for all my good luck. I am so lucky. It's so easy for me to have plenty of money. Travel experiences are flowing, fun and safe.

Malachite <mal-a-kite>

The swirling shades of green in malachite help to move the energy in your heart. The swirls create circles that appear like bull's eyes throughout the stone. This connects you to the ability to get to the heart of the issue using the focus of the bull's eye. If there are issues to be addressed and you recognize it's time to address them with no pussy-footing around, use malachite to aim your sights on uncovering and healing those issues.

Malachite Positive Thought Affirmation: I easily get to the heart of any matter. My heart is focused on love, light and well-being. Even when things appear to swirl around me, I am able to stay focused, loving both myself and others.

Rhodochrosite <row-doe-crow-sight>

Rhodochrosite is a stone to help you focus on love, and on happy, healthy friendships with friends and family. It helps you have faith, knowing you are loved and special!

Rhodochrosite has a high silver content. Some of the best specimens of rhodochrosite originate from Colorado and, in fact, it is their state stone. I visited the silver mines of Silverton in Colorado when I rode the Durango-Silverton Narrow Gauge Railroad. The miners often would cast away the rhodochrosite as the silver was mined. It was discarded due to the manganese content of the stone which was destructive to the processing of the silver. But gemstone collectors recognize the value of rhodochrosite!

Rhodochrosite Positive Thought Affirmation: I am love. I am balanced. My cells regenerate and rejuvenate in a healthy way.

Rose Quartz <rows courts>

The pastel pink vibration of rose quartz brings out love, comfort, compassion, tolerance, acceptance, warmth, care and well-being. This stone is the stone of gentle love which can be compared to the nurturing, safe and unconditional love of a mother. It is the essence of the heart chakra.

Use rose quartz to help you heal from loss – loss of love, loss of a friend or pet, loss in any sense. It nurtures you and supports you while you grieve your loss.

Rose quartz helps you manage feelings of anger and anxiety. It helps you feel calm and comforted. Rose quartz is a good stone for children. It's helpful for keeping away temper tantrums. It calms the spirit. Add it to your bedroom to promote peaceful sleep filled with loving vibrations.

Rose Quartz Positive Thought Affirmation: I am love. My life is filled with love, light and well-being. My skin and cells are healthy and rejuvenate daily. I am gentle and nurturing. I surround myself with people who are gentle and nurturing.

Unakite <oo-na-kite>

This pink and green stone is good for the heart and belly chakras. It opens the heart and balances the emotions. It is generally considered to be a balancing stone due to its nearly equal amounts of peachy pink and green colors. It is helpful when you feel moody.

Are you sometimes too hard on yourself? Do you feel like others are talking about you? Does that make you feel sad or nervous? Use unakite whenever you answer "yes" to these questions and when you are feeling and acting moody. Keep it nearby when you most need to have understanding and compassion for yourself and from others. Use unakite when you want to be more understanding and feel understood.

Unakite Positive Thought Affirmation: I am safe. All is well. Only goodness and joy are allowed in my energy field. I have compassionate understanding for myself and others. I am able to observe situations. I have a non-judgmental outlook.

Activity:

When can you benefit from using heart chakra stones? Choose the correct answer.

At school

At home

With friends

All of the above

5.
Light Blue Energy

Communication, angels and invisible helpers, honesty

Chakra: throat

Colors: sky blue, turquoise

Stones: angelite, aquamarine, amazonite, blue calcite, blue lace agate

Other stones for balance: carnelian, garnet, orange calcite

Keywords: communication, creative expression, truth, invisible helpers, angels, timing

The throat chakra is the place that helps you communicate, express, and really listen to others when they speak. The energy center at your throat and neck is like a doorway to your angels and invisible helpers. Most communication is received through your sight or your hearing, but you also receive information or messages that are a bit harder to define. These messages are often guidance from otherworldly beings like angels, your spirit guides, and friends and relatives who have passed away.

How does light blue energy feel?

Light blue is the color of the SKY. When you feel light blue energy you feel calm, peaceful and relaxed. When you are at ease, it is easy to say what you need to say. You are also able to hear what others are saying because it is easier to pay attention when you are calm.

Imagine you have light blue or turquoise in a bubble around you. In the bubble are feelings of peace. There are angels and invisible helpers in the blue energy that watch over you and guide you. You feel protected and connected to the Divine.

The sky blue energy helps you feel comfortable to speak up and say what you need to say. The light blue color helps you know that you are watched over by angels who will help you when you ask for their assistance.

Light blue energy in balance

You feel comfortable when you speak. You always have the right words to say. It is easy for you to stay focused on what other people are saying and you understand what they are talking about. It's easy for you to listen and hear. You trust intuitive messages and signs and apply them to your life. You are always on time and in the right place at the right time.

Too little light blue energy

You might feel misunderstood. You feel like people aren't listening to you. Your parents might be telling you to pay attention or that you aren't listening to them when they talk to you. You feel timid about speaking. You might realize that you aren't telling the whole truth or that you are lying to your parents or others. Or perhaps you can't seem to find the words to say what you mean. You might freeze up when the teacher calls on you, even if you know the answer. You might notice that you never seem to be in the right place at the right time.

Keep stones like amazonite, angelite, or blue lace agate in your pocket, desk or school bag. Use the light blue energy to help you find the words when you need to speak. Imagine there is an imaginary light blue band of energy around your neck that increases your ability to listen, understand, and to speak.

Too much light blue energy

You have too much blue energy if you are so calm and relaxed that you do nothing. If you are feeling very lazy or you procrastinate on your assignments, you might have too much light blue energy.

Imagine red and orange energy increasing your desire to get things done. Visualize the orange and red improving your ability to express yourself and transform the words and thoughts into action.

Balanced light blue energy helps you...

- communicate – talk comfortably with parents, teachers, friends.
- create – come up with new ideas, write stories and do art work.
- be in the right place at the right time.
- listen and hear well.
- connect with spirit guides and angels to receive their messages and guidance.
- develop intuition <in-too-ish-shun> through the senses of hearing, smell and taste.
- be truthful and honest.

The pastel blue energy of the throat chakra extends in a band of energy around the neck like a turtleneck sweater. It encompasses the area around the ears, nose and mouth. The energy is blue, like the color of the sky and turquoise.

Imagine angels and spirit guides always by your side helping you find the right words, helping you be exactly where you are supposed to be when you are supposed to be there. Let the blue energy help you speak honestly.

The opposite colors of red and orange can help motivate you or get you moving to get things done. Hold carnelian or garnet to move into action.

You can put a light blue or turquoise colored stone like amazonite or blue lace agate in your pocket or bag to help you speak up and always be honest in all you say and all you do. Use the light blue energy when you realize you aren't being totally honest with your friends or family, or when you can't seem to find the right words to speak or write. Try wearing light blue or turquoise clothes on days when have to give a speech, oral report, or need to talk to a friend about something. Use amazonite to help the truth be known about any situation.

Light blue stones help you to trust your inner voice or inner knowing, also known as intuition. Everyone has invisible friends or angels. These invisible helpers can assist and guide you. You are never alone!

Agate

As you know by now, agate gemstones come in many colors. Pair the color with the corresponding chakra to know its meaning. All agates are grounding, even the blue ones. When you are feeling jittery and need to be calm, then a blue lace agate will relax you as you hold it in your hand and think to yourself, "I am calm. I can do this." All blue stones can help you be calm and lessen the need to fight or be angry.

Blue lace agates stimulate good communication and connection with your guardian angel. Blue lace agate is a sky blue stone that grows naturally in that color and is not dyed by man to create the color.

Blue Lace Agate Positive Thought Affirmation: I express myself with ease and grace. I find the right words and have the courage to speak my truth.

Amazonite <A-may-za-night>

Amazonite is the stone of truth and honesty. Carry amazonite when you wish to know the truth of any issue. It provides the courage to know your truth, live your truth, speak your truth, and be your truth. You can use amazonite to attract people into your life who act with honesty and integrity. It also helps you communicate honestly and easily.

Amazonite Positive Thought Affirmation: I am surrounded by honest people of integrity. I live my truth and speak my truth with ease. I speak clearly. I easily find the words to express myself.

Angelite

This stone of the angels is the perfect stone to bring peace and calm into your life. The calming sky blue color gives you the feeling of peace. It helps you say what you need to say. It helps you understand what others are really saying. Communication involves being a good listener. Use angelite to improve your listening skills. True communication involves really understanding what the other person means when they speak.

Angelite helps you connect with your invisible friends – your angels, spirit guides, fairies, and what some people call your "imaginary friends". Your invisible helpers are always available to you and communicate with you whether or not you are consciously aware of it. They provide insight and clues through signs and symbols throughout your day. Angelite can help you become more aware of the messages being sent your way. Animals, birds and insects that appear on your path often bring messages. Look up the qualities and habits of the animal, bird or insect that shows up in your life. Angels and spirit guides inspire you with a thought or an idea, and then it is up to you to take action.

Angelite Positive Thought Affirmation: I am grateful to have all my Invisible Helpers assist me in my life. I live a charmed life. I am always in the right place at the right time. I am a good listener. I receive guidance and messages from my spirit guides and angels all the time!

Aquamarine

Aquamarine helps you communicate your feelings and emotions with self-confidence and ease. Aquamarine can help you understand the feelings you are having – even those feelings that are a bit hidden beneath the surface. Take some aquamarine into the bath or shower and form the intention to get in touch with the watery nature of your emotions. Make it your goal to become aware of your feelings. Allow any feelings that come, and decide it is safe to let disturbing emotions wash away.

The watery nature of aquamarine has connections with the sea, mermaids, and all sea life. Aquamarine is a wonderful amulet to give to a seafaring friend for boating, snorkeling or any seaworthy adventure.

Aquamarine Positive Thought Affirmation: I am in touch with my emotions and feelings. It is safe to feel my feelings. I express my feelings with ease and tact. I have safe voyages by sea and air. I am blessed with good communication skills.

Calcite

Calcite occurs in orange, blue, honey, brown, green, pink, red and clear. It also appears in different forms like masses or chunks, rhomboid and dogtooth formations.

Using blue calcite for the throat chakra can help you change how you communicate. It helps bring forth angelic assistance to guide your communication so that it may be filled with grace and tact.

Blue Calcite Positive Thought Affirmation: I express myself with ease, grace and fairness. I easily find the words I need, exactly when I need them, to say what needs to be said.

Activity:

Think about something you've wanted to say but have not said. Close your eyes. Use your imagination and make believe you are saying what you need to say. When you have finished visualizing and feel you have communicated all you need to share, draw a picture that represents how you feel.

6.
Dark Blue and Purple Energy

Inner knowing, intuition, telepathy

Chakra: third eye

Colors: purple, indigo blue

Stones: amethyst, blue goldstone, blue tiger's eye, lapis lazuli, purple-dyed agate, sodalite

Other stones for balance: clear quartz, citrine

Keywords: action, creativity, emotions, feelings

The third eye center, located behind the center of your forehead, is the primary spot to connect with your intuition and inner knowing. This is the energy center where it is easy for you to connect with your Higher Self – the part of you connected with the Universe, spirit guides and angels. This is the place where you know how to "see" the unseen, know the unknown, and feel that what isn't obvious. It is in the dark blue and purple energy that you connect with the invisible world of Spirit.

Intuition is your ability to know the truth regardless of any type of logic.

How does dark blue and purple energy feel?

Dark blue and purple energy is INTUITION and INNER KNOW-ING. You seem to know and have inner guidance that shows you truth. It is easy for you to access answers to any type of question within yourself.

Imagine you have a dark blue and purple bubble surrounding you. In the bubble are your guardian angels, invisible friends, messenger angels and spirit guides. Now imagine you are talking to them and listening to their guidance. You are feeling their love and support and you are able to use their help in your everyday life.

The colors dark blue and deep purple, and stones of those colors, help you believe in your own inner visions and that they can help you in your everyday life. The third eye center connects you to God, Goddess, saints, angels, and spirit guides. It can even help you connect with loved ones who have already passed away – including your pets. This energy center is also the place of intelligence and your ability to think clearly.

Dark blue and purple energy in balance

You feel connected to all life. You know the truth and have a deeper understanding of others. You receive great ideas. Sometimes you know things before they happen. You are connected with fairies, angels, and even those who have passed over. You feel divinely protected.

Too little blue and purple energy

You might feel like you don't understand what's going on around you. You feel out of balance and may misunderstand others. Maybe you don't connect to the feelings of others. Perhaps you can't get mentally clear enough to stay focused on the conversation or task at hand. You might feel agitated and frustrated. It is possible that you are having nightmares or are afraid of the dark.

Keep an amethyst or sodalite in your pocket by day and in your pillowcase by night. You can also keep purple or dark blue stones on the desk during the day and on the stand next to your bed with the idea that they will keep you clear-headed, safe, and calm.

Use stones like amethyst, purple-dyed agate, lapis lazuli, or blue tiger's eye.

Too much dark blue or purple energy

You might be feeling the feelings of others and it's uncomfortable. You might have a hard time knowing which feelings are yours and which feelings belong to someone else. You might feel angry or disturbed. Your heightened version of your senses might be a bit too much to handle.

Imagine the color purple and gold flowing around you. Place an amethyst or citrine in your hand. Connect with the feelings you are having and ask those feelings – "do you belong to me?" Look at the stone or rub the stone in your hand and have faith that you can determine what is true for you.

Use other stones for balance like citrine and clear quartz.

Balanced dark blue and purple energy helps you…
- think clearly and intelligently.
- access your intuition – your inner knowing that has all the answers you need.
- experience your psychic abilities through hearing, sight, feelings, knowing, smell and taste.
- balance your mind.
- use telepathy, the ability to read another's mind or thoughts. (Know what someone's saying or thinking about before they express it.)

Try visualizing a doorway or a portal behind the center of your forehead that brings you down a hallway to a safe, sacred space. This space is the part of you that is linked with your Higher Self – the part of you that is connected with the Universe, spirit guides and angels. Trust your intuition and your inner knowing. You were born with these abilities; have faith in your own feelings. These innate abilities are explained by the "six clairs":

Clairvoyance <clare-voy-ens> – intuitive sight through visions or dreams, like a daydream or something you can picture in your mind.

Clairaudience <clare-awe-dee-ens> – hearing through the intuition.

Clair cognizance <clare-cog-ni-sens> – knowing the truth for unexplainable reasons.

Clairsentience <clare-sent-ee-ens> –sensing the feelings of those around you.

Clairgustation <clare-gus-tae-shun> – receiving a message or idea through the sense of taste.

Clairolfaction <clare-ole-fact-shun> – sensing or knowing something because of a scent or a smell that other people can't smell.

All of these abilities are a heightened version of your sense of sight, hearing, knowing, feeling, tasting and smelling.

Telepathy is simply your ability to communicate by sending pictures from mind to mind.

When I was a little girl there were no cell phones or answering machines. My father was a builder so he was often out of the office. When my mother wanted my father to call home, we would close our eyes and imagine sending my father the idea of calling home. We would visualize him going to a phone and dialing the home phone number – thinking of each digit he would need to dial – and then imagine the phone ringing in the house. Then we would even imagine picking up the phone and saying, "Hi Daddy! Mommy wants to talk to you!" And it worked!

All the stones listed here can help with the challenges or qualities of the third eye center.

Agate

Use agate to ground your intuition and mental focus. Clear out the never-ending chatter of your mind with this stone. Use the dyed dark purple variety to activate your ability to go into a quiet state where thoughts slow down or stop. Intend to live your spiritual life and practice it in every aspect of your life through respect for nature, people and all things.

Purple-dyed Agate Positive Thought Affirmation: I am grounded in my spirituality. Spirituality is integrated into my daily life. I am intuitive and insightful. I am extremely intelligent.

Amethyst

Amethyst is great for changing any situation. It can help you shift a bad situation into a good one by focusing on what you want instead of the negative situation that is currently happening. It is associated with the breaking of bad habits. It helps you stay positive in your life.

Amethyst helps with dreaming good dreams and preventing nightmares. It will help you feel safe as you fall asleep at night.

Amethyst is also helpful for your imagination. Your imagination is a very good thing. Use it to create reality and dream big! Whatever you focus on, intensely desire and work diligently towards, *will* happen.

Amethyst Positive Thought Affirmation: I see, sense, feel and know life is magical. I dream pleasant dreams. I release all habits no longer for my highest good. I have a great connection with my spirit guides and angels. I am very intuitive. I trust my feelings.

Goldstone

There is a starry quality to goldstone that brings inner reflection as well as a reminder that you are a shining star. Gazing into goldstone reminds you to be all that you can be and allow your talents to shine brightly. The blue goldstone stimulates your third eye center with indigo midnight blue color to open your intuitive senses.

Blue Goldstone Positive Thought Affirmation: I am extremely intuitive. I receive messages from my guides and angels all the time. I am grateful for and trust my inner guidance.

Blue Tiger's Eye

This stone occurs in the colors of red and golden brown and is typically used at the solar plexus, navel and root centers. When it occurs in blue it is also known as Hawk's Eye. A hawk's vision is far and wide. A hawk can view life from a higher point. The hawk is also considered one of the messengers of Great Spirit in Native American spirituality.

The use of this stone can help you tune into messages from your angels, spirit guides, and deceased loved ones and maintain a vision of the bigger picture of life. It's an excellent tool for developing spiritual sight. Although it is a lofty stone, it is also a very grounding and protective stone. Remember, the golden brown brother of this tiger's eye is perfect for deflecting negative energy.

Blue Tiger's Eye Positive Thought Affirmation: I am able to visualize my reality into being. I am very insightful and have extraordinary moments of inspiration. I receive and interpret the messages from the heavenly realm all the time. I can see the bigger picture of life and act accordingly. I am grounded and protected in my spiritual development.

Lapis Lazuli <lap-iss la-zoo-lee>
The deep rich blue of lapis lazuli was used in ancient cultures as well as today. It provides peace, protection, grounding and insight into

the bigger picture of life. Lapis lazuli has been used since the ancient civilizations of legendary Atlantis and ancient Egypt. Today you will find it in jewelry, and tumbled stones you can carry in your pocket.

Use lapis lazuli for reducing pain, like migraines and headaches. It is also useful before and after surgery. Hold onto it if you get burnt. It helps calm anger and irritability. Use lapis to help you recover from upsets, like when you get so upset it causes a stomachache. Focus your attention on the positive aspects of life and you will feel better.

On a spiritual level, lapis lazuli can help you when you meditate or pray. Place it on your third eye, the center of your forehead, or hold it in your hand during meditation. It helps you when you want to imagine your fairies, angels or invisible friends.

Lapis Lazuli Positive Thought Affirmation: The wisdom of ancient cultures is stored within my cells, bones and muscles and I have access to it whenever I request it. I am extremely intuitive and receive messages and guidance all the time. I am calm and relaxed.

Sodalite <soda-light>

Sodalite is a rich royal blue stone. Sodalite is a component of lapis lazuli and much of the information about lapis also applies to sodalite. It is sometimes hard to tell the difference between the two stones. Just look for the pyrite flecks—if there are no flecks it is most likely sodalite.

Just like lapis, it reduces the frequency of migraines and headaches. It calms you down when you are upset, like when you feel angry or frustrated.

Sodalite Positive Thought Affirmation: I have calm emotions. My mind is clear and relaxed. I am intuitive. I am calm in my body, mind, and spirit. I feel balanced.

Activity:

Practice telepathy! Get together with a friend, sibling, or parent. Write down or draw an image on a piece of paper and fold it in four. Trade your paper with your partner but don't open it! Close your eyes, take some deep breaths and imagine, guess, or just know what is on the paper. Write down all the ideas that come to your mind while you are holding the paper. Nothing is too far out so write down everything that comes to mind – feelings, thoughts, visions, sensations. When you are both done, share the thoughts you had with each other. You will be pleasantly surprised with the results. Sometimes the information you receive doesn't have to do with what is on the paper but instead you might receive what is going on in the life of your partner in the exercise.

Unlimited potential, connection to God, higher intuition

Chakra: crown

Colors: white, purple, gold

Stones: amethyst, clear quartz, elestial, moonstone, selenite

Other stones for balance: black tourmaline, citrine, hematite, pyrite

Keywords: angels, miracles, connection to Higher Source, higher intuition

You are a spiritual being having a human experience. The crown chakra is at the very top of your head. It extends and goes beyond the top of your head and the energy creates a halo like a golden globe around your head. Can you imagine the halo you've seen in pictures of angels and saints? You have a halo, too!

You have unlimited potential. You were born with spiritual gifts. It is up to you to use them to help you in your life. As you learn to use these gifts, you can also use them to help and serve others. We each have the qualities of a miracle worker.

How does white energy feel?

White energy is the energy of the DIVINE or HEAVEN. You really know you can make your life and the lives of others better and better.

Imagine you have white light swirling around you. In the swirls are flecks of gold and violet. Feel your connection with angels, God, and the Divine. Remember you can communicate directly with the Higher Source. You feel the love and support of all that is good.

The colors white, violet, and gold, and stones of those colors, help you remember your connection to God. This energy center is also the place of intelligence and your ability to think clearly. It is the place where you communicate with the Divine.

White energy in balance

You know you are always Divinely protected. You have faith. You receive great ideas. You are smart. You know things and can't explain how you know or why you know. You know you have fairies, angels, and many loved ones who watch over you and guide you on your path. You feel divinely protected.

Too little white energy

You might feel disconnected and out of sorts. You feel vulnerable or alone in the world even when others are around. Maybe you are afraid. Sometimes you don't feel smart enough. You might feel agitated and frustrated. Sometimes you might have a dream that scares you. You might have forgotten that you are always protected and that you always have angels all around watching over you!

Keep an elestial or selenite nearby to remind you of your connections with the angels and the Divine. Place the selenite on your nightstand to help filter out scary dreams. Combine it with amethyst for protection and to create a feeling of safety. Take the time to hold the elestial and imagine your angels surrounding you so you become familiar with the feeling of angelic protection.

Use stones like amethyst, selenite and elestial (a type of quartz crystal).

Too much white energy

You rarely can have too much white light energy, but sometimes it can cause a feeling of being out of touch with living on Earth. You might feel so connected to the other realms that you forget to stay focused on tasks and being connected with your life as a student, sibling, or the child of your parents. You might feel spacey.

> *Imagine a laser beam of white light coming in through the crown of your head as you hold a piece of selenite in your hand. Place an amethyst tumbled stone or wand near your feet and imagine that the white light goes all the way to the tips of your toes. Continue to imagine white light roots growing from the soles of your feet so that you remain connected with Mother Earth. Be here now.*

Use other stones for balance like pyrite, hematite and black tourmaline.

Balanced white energy helps you...
- connect with Higher Source and angels.
- recognize and use your Higher Intuition.
- realize you have access to unlimited possibilities.
- create miracles and things that you *thought* were impossible.
- make spiritual connections.
- stay mentally balanced.

Higher intuition is when you know you are getting a direct message from angels or the Divine.

Belief in miracles, connection to a Higher Source, higher intuition, angels and fairies

The white energy of the crown chakra at the crown of the head expands like a globe of light or a halo. It encompasses the whole head. The energy is white with occasional rainbow lights.

You are a spiritual being having a human experience and the crown (top) of the head is the place where the connection is established. Like a portal, or a port on a computer, this is the physical place where the connection with the Divine is established. There are stones included here that are purple or violet because they are also helpful for the qualities of this energy center. These stones help you remember your connection with the heavenly realm and unlimited potential. You can be and do anything. Anything is possible!

Amethyst <am-a-thist>

This purple stone is part of the rainbow lights of your white halo. Amethyst is a crown chakra stone as well as a third eye stone. It gives you the power to alter negative situations. It helps you connect to the magic within you. Stay focused on your goals. Use your imagination to help you achieve anything your heart desires!

Amethyst can help you to change or transform all types of negative situations. Imagine yourself rolled up in a cocoon of purple light. The power of intending only good things shifts the vibration by using loving intentions. Love heals all situations.

Amethyst Positive Thought Affirmation: I now transform my life easily and with grace. I see, sense, feel and know that life is magical. I accept miracles within. I am with my spirit guides and angels. I am intuitive.

Clear Quartz

Clear quartz is silicon dioxide that forms into crystal points, clusters and masses. There are a variety of possible types of faces or facets on the point of this six-sided crystal. Clear quartz is found in veins in mountains around the world. It carries the full spectrum of light so in many ways it is good for anything you decide to use it for. Clear quartz is easily programmable with intention, which means it can literally hold information inside itself.

Clear quartz crystals help you stay focused and are excellent as amulets to use while you study. Carry the same crystal you used while studying when you take tests related to similar material. It will aid in memory and clarity of mind. Hold onto clear quartz when you need or want to gain clarity or certainty in any part of your life. Focus on the matter at hand and surround it with loving thoughts. Clear quartz will amplify your intention.

Clear Quartz Positive Thought Affirmation: I am focused in all that I do. I see life and situations clearly. I understand and know the answers when I need them.

Elestial <ee-lesst-chal>

Elestials are quartz crystals. They have multiple triangular faces. These "water crystals" are so named because they are found in riverbeds or in watery pockets of a mine. Some elestials have pockets of water inside and are sometimes called "enhydro" crystals, which simply means "with water." These quartz crystals offer you the opportunity to uncover deeper parts of your emotions and feelings so you can deal with them. With awareness, the emotions can be re-balanced using the crown's connection with the Divine.

Elestial Positive Thought Affirmation: My angels surround me and assist me all day, every day. I hear, I sense, I feel and I know guidance from my angels and spirit guides. I have balanced emotions. I am connected with ancient wisdom. Ancient wisdom is stored within me and I access it. I am inspired.

Moonstone

Moonstone comes in many colors including white, peach, beige, brown and black. When the light bounces off in such a way that it reveals rainbows within the stone, it is called rainbow moonstone. The reflective sheen from moonstone offers an avenue for developing a relationship with yourself.

Moonstone is also good to help you with your inner knowing. It helps with being intuitive, patient, thoughtful, nurturing, receptive, and calm.

Moonstone Positive Thought Affirmation: I allow love. I receive insight and wisdom. I flow with grace. I am thoughtful and calm.

Pyrite <pie-right>

Pyrite is an iron mineral that often crystallizes in the form of cubes. The golden vibration of pyrite assists you in remembering that you are amazing. It is good to use at your solar plexus for self-confidence and self-esteem. Pyrite is also helpful for the root chakra because it is grounding. Use it to activate your crown chakra to remind you of the golden flecks in your halo. With this stone in hand, visualize an energy field around your whole body, which is especially glowing around your head.

Pyrite Positive Thought Affirmation: My confidence is rock solid. I am focused on my intentions. I am connected to the shining light that I truly am. I take positive action to manifest my goals.

Selenite <sell-a-night>

This soft white gemstone, selenite, is strong and powerful for connecting the crown chakra with higher intuition, higher consciousness and the part of you that is the miracle worker. Its white coloring amplifies the white light in the halo part of your aura – the energy that surrounds your body – by increasing the brilliance.

Selenite is a tool for Reiki practitioners to aid in the alignment with Universal Life Force. Reiki is a Japanese technique used for stress reduction, relaxation and healing. Universal Life Force is another way of referring to the Divine, God, Goddess, Creator, Great Spirit.

Selenite realigns the spinal column when used with conscious intention. Use selenite when you meditate. Imagine white light filling your spinal cord. Selenite is good for the main structure of the body including muscles, tendons, ligaments and bones. It helps you connect with the ancient knowledge stored in the structure of your bones.

Selenite Positive Thought Affirmation: I am aligned with the Divine. I am a spiritual being of Divine Love and Divine Light. My spine, bones, tendons and muscles are healthy, strong and aligned.

Activity:

Try to list at least 3 times that you have felt angels or spiritual beings around you:

1. _____

2. _____

3. _____

How did that make you feel? _____

Would you like to feel that more often? _____

Why? _____

Why not? _____

From your pocket to your heart

These sparkling treasures are gifts from the Earth that become your tools. Use them with good thoughts to help you remember to always look at the positive in everything. These simple stones and this basic principle will help you be all that you can be and anything you can imagine. Use these beautiful stones to ignite the part of you that knows all you need to know. The magic of belief opens the door to everything. Be willing to try, and know that anything is possible!

May your life be filled with rainbow light and crystal blessings!

Glossary

ADHD (Attention-deficit/hyperactivity disorder). A chronic condition that affects millions of children and often persists into adulthood; includes some combination of challenges like difficulty sustaining attention, hyperactivity and impulsive behavior. Children with ADHD also may struggle with low self-esteem, troubled relationships and poor performance in school.

Affirmation. A positive thought or statement used to declare something to be true.

Angels. Luminous, bright and shining beings—neither masculine nor feminine—that act as Divine messengers. There are many types of angels, including Archangels, guardian angels, and many more. They act and react based on what you think or when you ask for help.

Amulet. Something that is meant to bring good luck and protection, can be made of practically any type of material.

Animal messages. The messages animals provide to help you understand something about yourself or a situation in your life. The use is associated with Native American spirituality and the spirituality of many indigenous people around the globe.

Animal totems. The essence of animal energy that aids you in your everyday life. Similar to spirit guides, animal totems energetically travel with you to help you with your spiritual quests.

Archangel. An angel of high rank.

Ascended Master. A spiritually aware being who has been born as a human being on the Earth in a past life or many past lives, such as St. Germain, Kuan Yin, Isis, or Walt Disney, to name a few.

Aura. The energy field around your body made up of your chakras and all your thoughts, feelings, emotions, beliefs, and words.

Autism. A mental condition, present from early childhood, characterized by great difficulty in communicating and forming relationships. A mental condition in which fantasy dominates over reality, as a symptom of schizophrenia and other disorders.

Chakra. A Sanskrit word for "wheel" or "vortex." The seven main chakras, or energy centers, that make up your physical, spiritual, mental and emotional bodies. They begin at the base of the spine with the root chakra and end at the head with the crown chakra, and all of them are actively connected.

Clairaudience. The ability to receive messages or guidance through intuitive hearing or sound that has not been produced by physical sound waves. The "voice within" is the connection to the Higher Self and to one's guides and angels.

Claircognizance. The ability to know something intuitively.

Clairgustation. The intuitive ability to recognize a taste in the mouth that provides insight into a matter at hand. Medical intuitives often use this sensory gift, or natural sense, to identify their clients' physical challenges.

Clairolfaction. The ability to intuitively pick up a smell that doesn't physically exist as scent, which provides some sort of guidance or clue into a situation at hand.

Clairsentience. The ability to clearly sense, or feel, and therefore know.

Clairvoyance. The ability to receive intuitive messages that come as visions in the mind's eye, including dreams and daydreams, through the vibration or energy of spiritual sight. This vibration exists primarily at the third eye.

Consciousness. A term used to explain awareness as it relates to oneself, the world around you and your inner world. Your beliefs and thoughts that are part of the natural thinking process.

Creativity. The use of the imagination or original ideas, especially in artistic work.

Discern. To recognize or understand by sight or inner knowing.

Eloquent. Able to speak well with confidence and sureness.

Empathy. The ability to understand and share the feelings of another.

Enlightened. Spiritually aware.

Folklore. Legends or stories that are passed down from one generation to another.

Grounded. To be focused and centered. Ability to concentrate and be present with the task at hand.

Igneous. Relates to a rock that solidified from lava or magma.

Indigenous. The native or original people of the Earth or an area.

Inflammation. Refers to swelling, irritation or anger. Often painful.

Intention. A purpose or course of action. A plan or goal.

Intuition. A thing that one knows without the need to know why you know.

Manifestation. An event, intention, action or object that clearly shows up in reality.

Meditation. A practice of quieting the mind. It's called a practice because it takes practice with every moment of the experience to stay focused on nothing.

Metamorphic. A rock that has undergone change by heat, pressure, or other natural means.

Metaphor. A figure of speech or a symbol that is used to represent, express or clarify something else in order to promote better understanding.

Metaphysical. Beyond the physical. This concept includes what the physical and scientific worlds cannot define yet clearly exists. Many of the principles and discussions within this book are metaphysical.

Opaque. Not able to see through. Not clear.

Spirit guides. Beings who exist in another dimensional reality that don't have a physical body. These guides become helpers when we make a clear decision to choose to invite them into our spiritual circle. It is important to choose your spirit guides wisely, just as you choose your friends wisely.

Telepathy. Communication without the use of the spoken word; a form of mental energy used for mind-to-mind and heart-to-heart communication.

Thoughtforms. Mental energy.
Visualization. A mental image that is similar to a visual perception. Visualizing is the creation of images in the mind.

Crystal Easy Reference

Agate, blue lace. Aids communication, speaking in front of groups, expression, good listening skills, help from your angels, trust in your inner voice, intuition, truth, integrity and honesty.

Agate, brown. Helps with grounding and getting down to earth, helps maintain focus, calms, releases feelings of anger and frustration, promotes feeling safe and secure, helps motivation to finish homework, chores and school projects.

Agate, green-dyed. Opens your heart, helps you make good friends and keep good friends, activates a general feeling of well-being, helps you to see the good in all things, connects you with nature spirits, and is associated with gardening.

Agate, pink. Promotes joy, happiness, good friends, supportive family, good relationships with all people and animals. Encourages empathy or feeling compassion for someone, understanding. Helps you stay positive and see the good in all things.

Agate, purple. Increases intuition, magnifies insight and understanding, improves study skills and memory retention, brings clarity of mind, helps with thinking through challenging problems, helps with balancing mental states.

Amazonite. Brings courage to speak your truth, honesty, integrity, clear communication, eloquence, creative expression. Improves singing abilities, speaking in front of groups, helps with listening skills. Promotes angelic connections, Divine intervention, help from your angels.

Amber. Safety, healthy boundaries, protection, feeling cared for and nurtured, connection with trees, confidence, joyfulness. Helps you remember your magnificence and maintain your sacred space.

Amethyst. Helps you change things for the better, break bad habits, fall asleep at night, remember your dreams and prevent nightmares.

Improves imagination and intuition, makes your spiritual connection stronger, helps communication with spirit guides and angels.

Angelite. Improves communication and listening skills, aids angelic communication and guidance, improves insight and intuition.

Apache tears. Protects, helps you when you are sad, good for grieving the death of a loved one or a pet. Grounds, calms, comforts, useful for staying focused, promotes feelings of safety and security. Aids connection to Native American spirituality and other indigenous cultures.

Apatite. Good for digestion or a stomachache, helps with eating disorders, balances your appetite, helps maintain proper weight, encourages supportive friends and family, helps you establish boundaries with others.

Aquamarine. Helps with communication of feelings, promotes creativity through Divine inspiration, balances emotions, improves connection with the angels. Aids swimming, boating, and all other water-associated activities.

Aventurine, green. Good for luck and travel. The stone of good fortune. Increases good health, promotes a willingness to get along with others.

Calcite, blue. Brings courage and balances emotions. Helps with anxiety and accepting change. Promotes creativity, physical strength, strong bones and muscles.

Calcite, orange. Calms muscle spasms, relieves pain, strengthens bones, good for physical education class and sports, aids with balancing emotions and feelings, calms anxiety associated with change, promotes creativity, good for artists and musicians, improves courage and optimism.

Calcite, pink. Promotes love, kindness, compassion, acceptance, tolerance. Nurtures, comforts, opens you to believe in miracles, helps you make good friends, aids in relationships – both romantic and platonic.

Carnelian. Brings creativity, motivation, courage. Helps you complete tasks, balances anger, improves breathing, helpful for asthmatic conditions and arthritis.

Chrysocolla. Increases inner peace and calm, heals anger, balances emotions and hurt feelings; decreases agitation, frustration, aggravation and inflammations.

Chrysoprase. Provides soothing and nurturing energy, helps heal a broken heart, offers joy and empathy. Useful when you need to understand the actions of others, increases your ability to see the good in all things.

Citrine. Brings joy, optimism, self-esteem, courage, mental clarity, insight. Helps you overcome fears and feel safe to be powerful.

Elestial. Balances emotions, encourages connection with angels and the Divine, improves brain function and memory, aids in accessing inner wisdom.

Garnet. Improves motivation and eliminates procrastination or putting off till tomorrow what you can do today, aids in bringing your ideas into reality, improves physical endurance and overall health and well-being.

Goldstone, blue. Opens your intuitive senses, helps you connect with your inner guidance. Aids communication with the Divine, angels and guides.

Goldstone, green. Activates your ability to love yourself and others, reminds you to be grateful, increases abundance and prosperity, attracts things you really want.

Goldstone, red. Helps you shine your light and remember your magnificence, helps you improve talents and skills, encourages enthusiasm, improves your emotions.

Hematite. Grounding, calming, helpful for ADD/ADHD. Helps you focus, relieves frustration and agitation, lowers blood pressure, reduces muscle cramps, helps you let go of worry and fear, and brings feelings of well-being.

Jasper, dalmatian. Promotes loyalty, authentic friendships, unconditional love. Increases the ability to be able to tell when someone is being real and a good friend.

Jasper, red. Stone of motivation and taking action. Amplifies strength and endurance, increases vitality or energy, brings an ability to accomplish a lot, helps with focus and grounding.

Jasper, yellow. Encourages feeling safe to shine your light, increases courage and self-confidence, grounds the idea of having a strong sense of self, improves self-esteem, helps you achieve anything you put your mind to.

Lapis lazuli. Provides peace, protection, calm, focus, grounding, access to the wisdom of the ages. Good for meditation. Reduces inflammation and burns; good for arthritis, headaches and migraines.

Malachite. Helps with digestion and diabetes, eases stomachaches, heals hurt feelings, provides the ability to get to the heart of a matter, realigns you with the sweetness of life.

Moonstone. Brings forth ancient wisdom from within, good for developing your intuition and extrasensory perception. Use to connect with the moon cycles, balance hormones and ease their symptoms.

Obsidian, black. Helps with grounding or getting down to earth, protects, deflects negativity, promotes a sense of safety and helps you focus.

Obsidian, golden sheen. Helps prevent arguments, increases protective energy, improves your ability to think happy thoughts and attract goodness and love in your life.

Obsidian, rainbow. Reminds you to see the full spectrum of light even within the darkness, acts as a mirror to your soul, deflects negativity, draws in goodness and love, rebalances turbulent emotions.

Obsidian, snowflake. Helps you see the good within all things, reduces fear of the unknown and fear of the darkness, grounds, balances, helpful for ADD/ADHD.

Peridot. Helps remove anger and jealousy, adds healing vibrations, encourages you during hard times, aids with digestion.

Quartz, clear. Aids memory, focus, clear intention. Helpful for everything as you can charge it with your intention. Good for studying and taking tests.

Rhodochrosite. Stone of self-love, healthy relationships, and finding the silver lining. Promotes healthy cells, improves ability to regenerate and rejuvenate (rebuild) the body, amplifies love and self-empowerment.

Rose quartz. Stone of unconditional love. Amplifies acceptance and tolerance, provides comfort and support, attracts love, projects love, reduces anger and jealousy.

Selenite. Connection to God and the angels. Improves the energy of your aura and increases positive vibrations, Reiki healer's stone. Improves physical structure. Athlete's stone.

Sodalite. Invokes feelings of peace and calm, helpful for headaches, reduces inflammations, repels anger and frustration, increases inner wisdom.

Tiger's eye, blue. Helps you see situations from different perspectives, opens your spiritual ears to receive messages from Spirit, increases ability to see and understand symbols in dreams and daily life, grounds, protects, good for eyesight.

Tiger's eye, gold. Repels negativity and jealousy, increases self-esteem and courage, helps you invoke feelings of safety, improves ability to set boundaries.

Tiger's eye, red. Repels negativity, increases self-motivation, improves vital energy, increases courage and the ability to take action, helps you complete tasks.

Tourmaline, black. Wards off negativity, reduces effects of electromagnetic frequencies, refocuses your energy. Good to help rebalance, helps you get your homework done, and reduces distractions.

Unakite. Stone of the balanced emotions. Increases feelings of comfort and safety, improves acceptance and repels feelings of judgment and jealousy, helps you love yourself. An ally for loving relationships – both friendly and romantic.

Life Challenges Easy Reference

Argument with parents. Amethyst, blue lace agate, chrysocolla, lapis lazuli, rose quartz, sodalite

Afraid of the dark. Amethyst, brown agate, black tourmaline, clear quartz, garnet, hematite, jasper, selenite, sodalite, tiger's eye

Acceptance by your classmates. Citrine, pink calcite, rhodonite, rose quartz, tiger's eye

Bad dreams. Amethyst, angelite, black tourmaline, blue lace agate, elestial, rose quartz, selenite

Being aggressive or out of control. Amethyst, blue lace agate, black tourmaline, blue calcite, hematite, sodalite, lapis lazuli

Bullying – for both the victim and the bully. Amethyst, angelite, black tourmaline, citrine, green aventurine, hematite, orange calcite, peridot, rhodochrosite, rose quartz, tiger's eye

Clash with best friend. Amethyst, angelite, chrysocolla, clear quartz, chrysoprase, green goldstone, green calcite, malachite, pink calcite, rhodochrosite, rose quartz, unakite

Concentration in class. Agate, amethyst, black tourmaline, clear quartz, citrine, blue tiger's eye, lapis lazuli, purple-dyed agate, pyrite, hematite, sodalite

First day of school or first day in a new school. Citrine, clear quartz, hematite, lapis lazuli, rose quartz, orange calcite, pyrite, sodalite, yellow jasper

Heartsick from grief or loss of love. Amethyst, apache tears, black tourmaline, pink calcite, rhodonite, rhodocrosite, rose quartz

Shyness. Amazonite, angelite, carnelian, citrine, clear quartz, hematite, malachite, orange calcite, rose quartz, yellow jasper

Self-confidence. Amber, amethyst, apatite, citrine, goldstone, jasper, malachite, peridot

Speaking in front of class. Angelite, amazonite, aquamarine, blue calcite, blue lace agate, citrine, clear quartz, carnelian, elestial, hematite, selenite

Taking a test – for memory and nervousness. Blue calcite, clear quartz, citrine, hematite, lapis lazuli, selenite, sodalite

Timing – Being on time, waking up or showing up for school and appointments. Angelite, blue lace agate, clear quartz, elestial, hematite, lapis lazuli, selenite, sodalite

Bibliography

Andrews, Ted. *Animal-Speak: The Spiritual and Magical Powers of Creatures Great and Small.* Woodbury, MN: Llewellyn Publications, 1993.

Andrews, Ted. *Animal-Wise: The Spirit Language and Signs of Nature.* Jackson, TN: Dragonhawk, 1999.

Gardner-Gordon, Joy. *Color and Crystals: A Journey through the Chakras.* Feasterville Trevose, PA: Crossing Press, 1988.

Hay, Louise. *Heal Your Body.* Carlsbad, CA: Hay House, 1984.

Lembo, Margaret Ann. *Chakra Awakening: Transform Your Reality Using Crystals, Color, Aromatherapy and the Power of Positive Thought.* Llewellyn, 2011.

Melody. *Love is in the Earth: A Kaleidoscope of Crystals; The Reference Book Describing the Metaphysical Properties of the Mineral Kingdom.* Wheat Ridge, CO: Earth-Love, 1991.

Milanovich, Norma, and Shirley McCune. *The Light Shall Set You Free.* Scottsdale, AZ: Athena, 1996.

Raphaell, Katrina. *Crystal Enlightenment: The Transforming Properties of Crystals and Healing Stones.* Vol. 1. Santa Fe, NM: Aurora Press, 1985.

Raphaell, Katrina. *Crystal Healing: The Therapeutic Application of Crystals and Stones.* Vol. 2. Santa Fe, NM: Aurora Press, 1987.

Raphaell, Katrina. *Crystalline Transmission: A Synthesis of Light.* Vol. 3. Santa Fe, NM: Aurora Press, 1990.

Sams, Jamie. *The 13 Original Clan Mothers: Your Sacred Path to Discovering the Gifts, Talents & Abilities of the Feminine Through the Ancient Teachings of the Sisterhood.* New York, NY: HarperCollins Publishers, 1993.

Shinn, Florence Scovel. *The Writings of Florence Scovel Shinn.* 4th ed., Camarillo, CA: DeVorss, 1996.

Ywahoo, Dhyani. *Voices of Our Ancestors: Cherokee Teachings from the Wisdom Fire.* Boston, MA: Shambhala Publications, Inc. 1987.

Picture Credits

All crystal photographs inside the book © Andy Frame 2012 / www.andyframe.com, except p. 101 (selenite) © Ines Blersch 2003; p. 49 (rough citrine) © Linda/shutterstock.com; p. 97 © Zaneta Baranowska/shutterstock.com, p. 18 (illustration), and chakra symbols throughout © Viktoria/shutterstock.com.

Index

Please also check pages 103-109 for more information on your search subject!

EARTHDANCER

A FINDHORN PRESS IMPRINT